The Best Of
JIM BRICKMAN

ARRANGED BY DAN COATES

Project Managers:
Carol Cuellar &
Jeannette DeLisa
Art Layout:
Joann Carrera

Contents

6)   ANGEL EYES

12)   BORDERS

9)   BY HEART

16)   HEARTLAND

24)   HERO'S DREAM

28)   IF YOU BELIEVE

32)   PICTURE THIS

19)   ROCKET TO THE MOON

36)   SHAKER LAKES

40)   VALENTINE

Dan Coates

One of today's foremost personalities in the field of printed music, Dan Coates has been providing teachers and professional musicians with quality piano material since 1975. Equally adept in arranging for beginners or accomplished musicians, his Big Note, Easy Piano and Professional Touch arrangements have made a significant contribution to the industry.

Born in Syracuse, New York, Dan began to play piano at age four. By the time he was 15, he'd won a New York State competition for music composers. After high school graduation, he toured the United States, Canada and Europe as an arranger and pianist with the world-famous group "Up With People".

Dan settled in Miami, Florida, where he studied piano with Ivan Davis at the University of Miami while playing professionally throughout southern Florida. To date, his performance credits include appearances on "Murphy Brown," "My Sister Sam" and at the Opening Ceremonies of the 1984 Summer Olympics in Los Angeles. Dan has also accompanied such artists as Dusty Springfield and Charlotte Rae.

In 1982, Dan began his association with Warner Bros. Publications - an association which has produced more than 400 Dan Coates books and sheets. Throughout the year he conducts piano workshops nation-wide, during which he demonstrates his popular arrangements.

ANGEL EYES

Composed by
JIM BRICKMAN
Arranged by DAN COATES

Angel Eyes - 3 - 1

8

Angel Eyes - 3 - 3

BY HEART

Composed by
JIM BRICKMAN and
HOLLYE LEVEN
Arranged by DAN COATES

Lyrics:

Hold me close, ___ ba — by, ___ please.
When you go, ___ I'll stop ___ the clock.

Tell me an — y-thing but that you're gon — na leave.
I won't ev — er let this mo — ment stop.

As I kiss ___ this fall — en tear, ___ I pro — mise you I will be ___
Time is steal — in' you from me, ___ but it can nev — er take this mem — o-

BORDERS

Composed by
JIM BRICKMAN
Arranged by DAN COATES

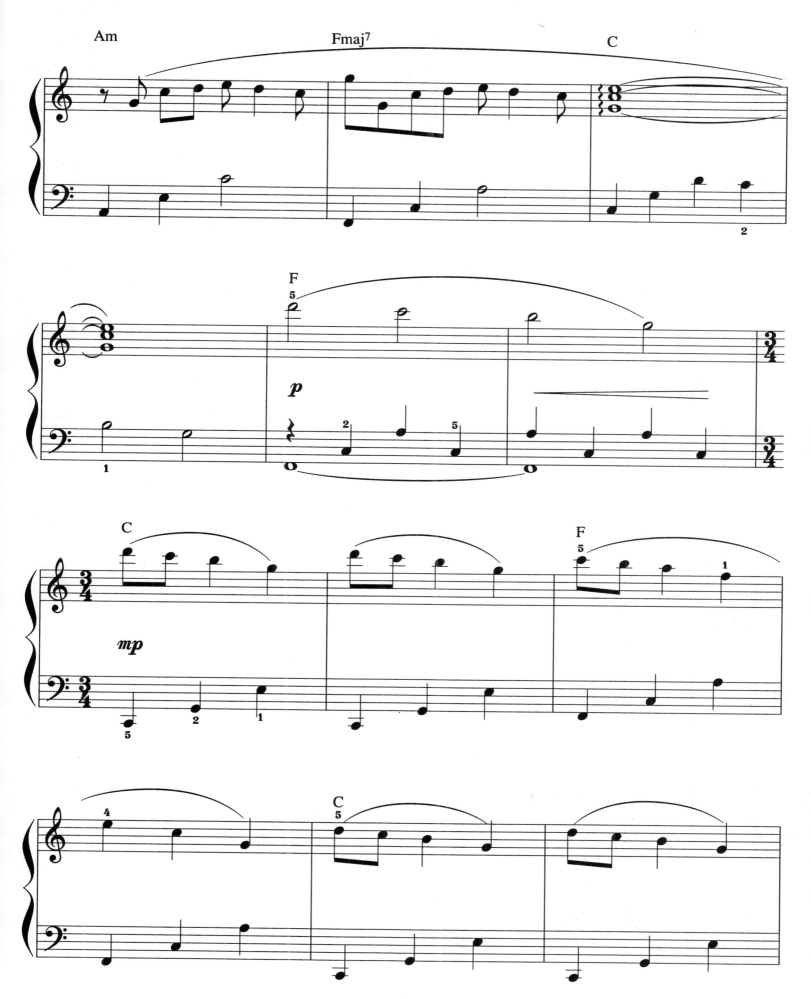

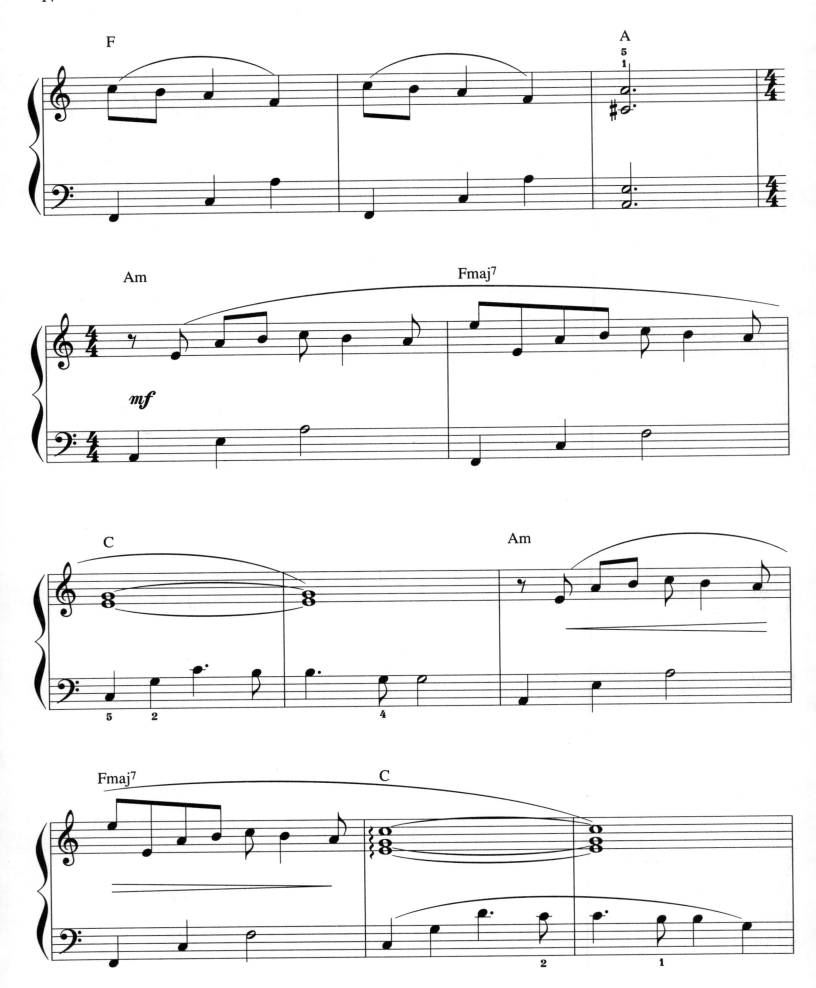

14

HEARTLAND

Composed by
JIM BRICKMAN and ELLEN WOHL
Arranged by DAN COATES

ROCKET TO THE MOON

Composed by
JIM BRICKMAN
Arranged by DAN COATES

20

22

Rocket to the Moon - 5 - 5

HERO'S DREAM

Composed by
JIM BRICKMAN
Arranged by DAN COATES

Hero's Dream - 4 - 4

IF YOU BELIEVE

Composed by
JIM BRICKMAN
Arranged by DAN COATES

PICTURE THIS

Composed by
JIM BRICKMAN
Arranged by DAN COATES

Picture This - 4 - 2

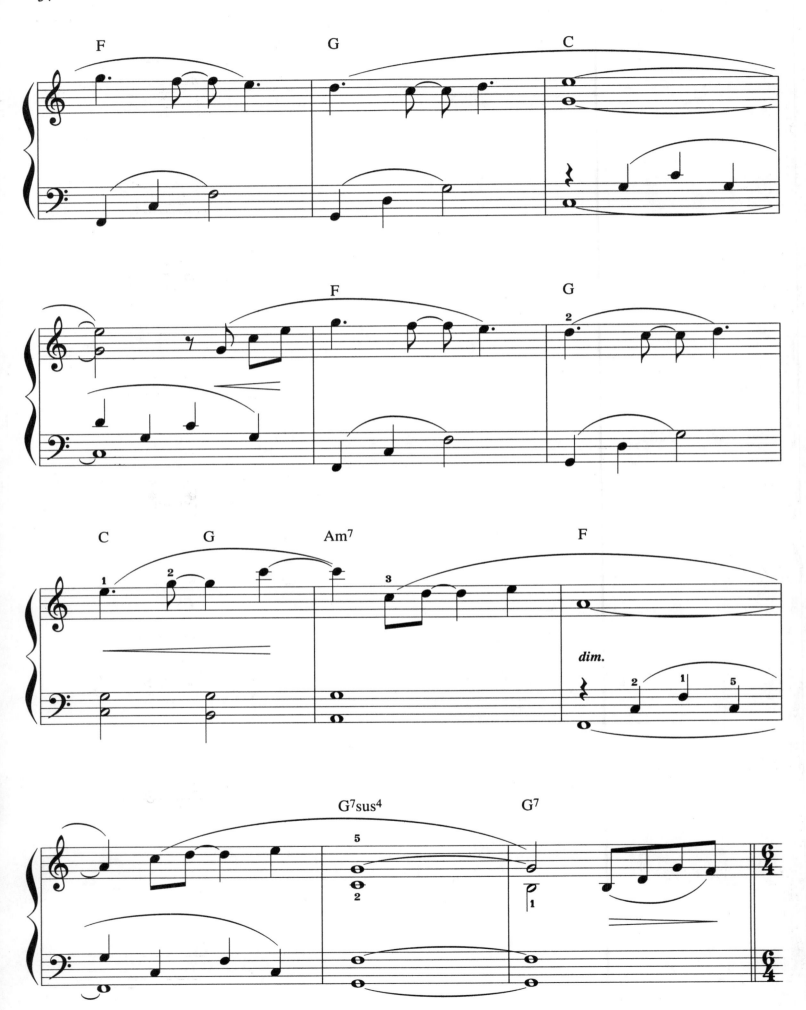

Picture This - 4 - 4

SHAKER LAKES

Composed by
JIM BRICKMAN
Arranged by DAN COATES

Shaker Lakes - 4 - 2

Shaker Lakes - 4 - 4

VALENTINE

Composed by
JIM BRICKMAN and JACK KUGELL
Arranged by DAN COATES

Valentine - 4 - 2

Verse 2:
All of my life,
I have been waiting for all you give to me.
You've opened my eyes
And shown me how to love unselfishly.
I've dreamed of this a thousand times before,
But in my dreams I couldn't love you more.
I will give you my heart until the end of time.
You're all I need, my love,
My Valentine.

WINDHAM HILL RECORDINGS BY OR FEATURING

JIM BRICKMAN

INCLUDE:

SOLO ALBUMS:
NO WORDS
BY HEART
PICTURE THIS

COMPILATIONS:
PIANO SAMPLER 2
A WINTER SOLSTICE V
WINDHAM HILL SAMPLER 1996
THE CAROLS OF CHRISTMAS

JIM BRICKMAN would like to invite you to be on his Mailing List to receive information about concert schedules, merchandise and upcoming releases. Please fill out the coupon below and mail to:

JIM BRICKMAN
c/o EDGE ENTERTAINMENT
11288 VENTURA BLVD. SUITE 606
STUDIO CITY, CA 91604

(818) 508-8400 phone
(213) 876-6815 fax
        or
E-Mail us at BrickPiano@AOL.com. or call 1-888-BRICKMAN for **VIP Club Membership**, concert tour and merchandise information.
Find Jim Brickman's Web Page at www.Windham.com.

Cut Along Here ✂

NAME _____

ADDRESS _____

CITY_____ STATE _____ ZIP_____

DOB:_____ E-Mail _____

Phone:_____

I first heard about Jim Brickman's music _____

The Best Of Jim Brickman — Easy Piano (Coates)